Perhaps nothing is more human than to assume that things easily seen are more real and important than those largely hidden from view. Take icebergs, for example. Typically, we focus on the highly visible tips of icebergs above the water's surface rather than the much larger masses of ice hidden from us under the cold, dark water. We fail to appreciate how much the tip depends on all of that mass below it in order to float and how much additional mass is hidden from our view.

Photo REmoved Due to Copyright Restrictions

Titanic **iceberg**. (From Wikimedia Commons, accessed 3 June 2014, http://commons
.wikimedia.org/wiki/File:Titanic_iceberg.jpg.)

In many ways, it's the same story with Air Force command and control (C2). Over the last couple of decades, the US Air Force has pioneered and developed a C2 enterprise for joint and coalition airpower that is rivaled by none.[1] When we describe it, we tend to emphasize the highly visible aspects of tactical employment, like the mission-package coordination and tactical execution activities practiced in every Red Flag exercise.[2] As one would expect, however, there is much, much more to the C2 story in terms of who created the plan and whether it will contribute to our desired strategic outcomes.

As we make difficult choices in an era of reduced resources, we must ensure that we do not lose sight of the people, processes, and ideas that help link our tactical actions to desired strategic outcomes. This article describes the foundational C2 concepts that comprise the "entire C2 iceberg." After a brief discussion of the more familiar "tip of the C2 iceberg," it then addresses "the rest of the C2 iceberg"—the people, processes, and products that constitute the air tasking cycle in component major command and numbered air force headquarters. For our purposes—and to suggest a useful distinction not discriminatingly demarcated in Air Force C2 doctrine—the article refers to these as component headquarters command and control (CHQ C2). It lays out current threats to CHQ C2, including cognitive traps, systemic factors, *and "systems illiteracy," all of which currently work to weaken our entire C2 system design*—and, ultimately, our strategic performance—from within. Finally, the article discusses what can be done to ensure that the Air Force's operational-level C2 skills maintain pace with our tactical prowess, assuring that this prowess—as well as the Air Force itself—remains relevant in future security environments.

The Whole Iceberg: Fundamental Functions of C2

Military historian Martin van Creveld observed, "As even a cursory look at their nature will reveal, the functions of command are eternal. Provided he had a force of any size at his disposal, a stone-age chieftain would be confronted with every single one of them, just as is his present day successor."[3] A functional approach to C2 system design anchors planners in the fundamentals of *what* must be done in C2 operations before getting specific about *how* to do it or *who* should do it. In a metaphorical sense, let us lift the entire C2 iceberg, step back far enough to see the whole thing, and describe what it does.

According to Joint Publication (JP) 1-02, *Department of Defense Dictionary of Military and Associated Terms*, command and control is "the exercise of authority and direction by a properly designated commander over assigned and attached forces in the accomplishment of the mission."[4] Thus, the two most essential elements are (1) a commander who has the authority to assign missions and direct forces to accomplish them and (2) a system through which the commander can control his or her forces to carry out that mission.

Commanders exercise command through use of a C2 system, defined in JP 1-02 as "the facilities, equipment, communications, procedures, and personnel essential to a commander for planning, directing, and controlling operations of assigned forces pursuant to the missions assigned."[5] Thus, the design of a C2 system must concentrate on serving the needs and requirements of the commander and the mission. The system's design must have the ability to flex to both the individual commander's specific requirements and the ever-changing mission environment. As described in the 1989 RAND study *Command Concepts: A Theory Derived from the Practice of Command and Control*, the essence of C2 is developing, transmitting, and executing the "command concept," which only the commander has the authority to develop and promulgate:

> Going beyond personality alone, . . . the essence of command lies in the cognitive processes of the commander—not so much the way certain people do think or should think as the ideas that motivate command decisions and serve as the basis of control actions: Ideally, the commander has a prior concept of impending operations that cues him (and his C2 system) to look for certain pieces of information. Our theory cuts through the technological overlay that now burdens the subject . . . [and] represents an attempt to separate the intellectual performance of the commander from the technical performance of the C2 system.[6]

In other words, the critical minimum infrastructure of a holistic C2 system cannot be determined generically or agnostically; rather, it is entirely dependent upon the commander's requirements, given specific missions to accomplish under specific conditions. This C2 system is then used to translate the specific command concept into meaningful, collective action.

Holistic C2 systems, however constructed, must be adequate to match the needs of the commander, whose responsibility can range from very small areas of interest in the case of a highly specialized task force to the breadth of the entire globe in the case of a functional combatant command. At a minimum, they must

- *build situational awareness* (keep the commander and staff informed of the current situation and his/her guidance from higher headquarters);

- *translate commander's intent* (assist the commander in the development and communication of the command concept [which includes both their organizational and operational concepts]);

- *produce feasible plans* (disseminate the command concept to subordinates in clear and unambiguous terms); and

- *conduct mission control* (be sufficient to monitor and control the execution actions of subordinates to the minimum degree required to accomplish the commander's concept, and to allow the commander to issue new instructions when the situation and/or the commander's concept changes).

Any discussion of holistic C2 systems, under contested conditions or otherwise, will concentrate on supporting these most basic functions. It is the job of the commanders and the staff to build and adapt the C2 system to meet those parameters in each case, and there is seldom only one feasible and acceptable way to do it. No matter how it is done, the C2 system serves as an extension of the commander and thus can never be divorced from human interaction.

"The Tip" versus "the Rest" of the C2 Iceberg

When we talk about C2 in the context of Air Force tactical employment, we usually have in mind the C2 elements that execute the air tasking order (ATO)—the Airborne Warning and Control system (AWACS), Joint Surveillance Target Attack Radar System (JSTARS), control and reporting center (CRC), air support operations center (ASOC), and air and space operations center (AOC) combat operations division (COD).[7] Typically, personnel receive training in these elements during common exercises such as Red Flag (live fly) and Virtual Flag (simulated flight environments), in which we sharpen our execution tactics, techniques, and procedures. The C2 elements above—the ones focused on executing the current plan in real time—can be thought of as the tip of our metaphorical C2 iceberg. They serve as connections to the larger C2 system that almost all operators became familiar with early in their initial tactical assignments. Other vital actions support employment (e.g., space enhancement and cyber activities), but this article examines the central tasking processes for air-breathing assets.

The rest of the iceberg includes everything that produces the overarching plan which allows commanders to translate their strategy into the operations and tasks that will fulfill the mission. The rest of the iceberg creates the conceptual and logistical underpinnings of the joint campaign executed by mission commanders at the tip of the iceberg. This requires a blend of operational art and science as well as the ability to negotiate complex bureaucratic environments.[8] C2 systems literacy—the construction of sufficiently accurate individual and collective mental models of the world with which to take useful action—involves understanding the whole C2 iceberg and the dynamic organizational processes that keep it afloat (see the figure below).

Figure. The C2 iceberg (notional). (From Shutterstock, http://www.shutterstock .com/pic.mhtml?id=131163173&src=id, adapted for this article in accordance with the licensing agreement, http://www.shutterstock.com/licensing.mhtml.)

AAMDC - US Army Air and Missile Defense Command

AETF - air expeditionary task force

AFFOR - Air Force forces

AOC - air operations center

AOD - air operations directive

ASOC - air support operations center

ATO/ACO - air tasking order / airspace control order

AWACS - Airborne Warning and Control System

BCD - battlefield coordination detachment

CC - component commander

C-MAJCOM/C-NAF - component major command / component numbered air force

COCOM - combatant command

CRC - control and reporting center

DIRMOBFOR - director of mobility forces

DIRSPACEFOR - director of space forces

ISR - intelligence, surveillance, and reconnaissance

(J)ACCE - joint air component coordination element

JAOP - joint air operations plan

JPRC - joint personnel recovery center

JSTARS - Joint Surveillance Target Attack Radar System

JTF - joint task force

MARLO - Marine liaison officer

MISREP - mission report

NALE - naval and amphibious liaison element

OGA/IA - other governmental agency / international agency

OPORD - operation order

OPTASKLINK - operations task link

ROE - rules of engagement

SOLE - special operations liaison element

SPINS - special instructions

TACREP - tactical report

TST - time sensitive target

In the US Air Force, the rest of the iceberg deals with component major command or component numbered air force processes that support specific geographic and functional combatant commanders.[9] These can be described generically as the component headquarters or CHQ, each of which has an Air Force forces (AFFOR) commander and staff who present forces to the joint force commander and deal with Air Force service-specific issues as a "force provider." It also includes the AOC, with the trained and proficient core of a joint or coalition air operations center (JAOC/CAOC) staff.[10] When the joint task force (JTF) commander establishes functional components, the joint force air component commander (JFACC) uses the jointly manned JAOC/CAOC to perform operational missions as a "force consumer." The commander of Air Force forces is always an Air Force commander and typically "dual hatted" as the JFACC although a JFACC can be an Airman from any service. Furthermore a JAOC should always be jointly manned with augmentees from the other service and coalition components. In practice, it is not unusual for the deputy JFACC to be an aviator from another service or coalition military partner. Air Force operational forces are normally presented to the joint force as an air expeditionary task force (AETF) in accordance with joint and service doctrine.[11]

The organizational skills required of commanders and their staffs to perform well in the rest of the iceberg are not the same as those tactical skills needed to succeed in the tip although having an in-depth understanding of tip activities is absolutely critical to building feasible plans in the rest of the iceberg.[12] Practitioners of CHQ C2 must be able to think beyond their tactical "family of origin" weapons systems and understand how the various joint and coalition forces can fit together into a coherent scheme of maneuver. Air planners in the JAOC are specifically trained in the joint operation planning process for air but also support the parallel joint operation planning process performed by JTF headquarters.[13] Thus, they must be familiar with multiple joint and functional operational-art concepts, doctrine, and terms. Moreover, they must be able to translate between them as they produce air component supporting plans to the joint campaign.[14] CHQ planners must work with various embedded liaisons from other agencies to coordinate integrated planning. Above all, they must focus these processes on getting the right decision-quality information to the appropriate commanders, who then use the same system to assess the situation, choose courses of action, accept risk, disseminate their guidance, and assign concrete tasks to the tactical units in the tip.

Just as one must understand aerodynamics, engineering, thermodynamics, computer science, and more when designing and operating aircraft, so must people who design and operate C2 systems grasp the organizational theories and concepts inherent to CHQ C2. They must be versed in group decision-making theories, jargon used in operational graphics and orders production, war gaming, operational analysis, communications network architecture, and information security. These concepts, and many others not detailed here, are like the crystalline structure upon which the collective strength of the entire C2 iceberg depends.

These people, processes, and tools of CHQ C2 bring predictability, rigor, and discipline to the air tasking cycle, which is very important to a process in which seemingly minute details can often have a disproportionately large impact on effectiveness during execution. They enable the detailed integration of many assets from many locations, help to eliminate costly resource mismatches and targeting errors, identify operational limits, and create the cognitive and logistical backbone of the plan that the COD and its subordinate tactical C2 elements can then modify as needed on the day of execution. Shortcutting this process may be necessary at times or even desirable, but doing so almost always comes with additional costs in a systemic sense: it usually increases strategic and operational risk when careful target analysis and weaponeering, requirements resourcing, deconfliction of friendly forces, synchronization of supporting effects, collateral damage estimates, and so forth, are abbreviated or omitted for the sake of operational urgency. For very good reasons, these processes and procedures have withstood the test of time and should be the entering argument for the evolution of our C2 systems. Those who fail to understand the holistic nature of the system when offering alterative solutions risk introducing internal threats to our C2 excellence.

Threats to C2 Excellence

Complacency in C2 System Design

Often, long periods of success without serious challenge lead to complacency. When something is done well for a long period with few notable mishaps, the human tendency is to forget lessons previously learned, become comfortable, and assume that the future will closely resemble the past. When this happens, it becomes very difficult to recognize game-changing events in the operational environment—that is, until it is too late. Four conditions that we have collectively become accustomed to over decades of deployed combat operations may lead to cognitive complacency in the design and maintenance of C2 systems.

The "recent" operational environments have been largely static and predictable compared to likely future conflicts. The Air Force can be proud of the service provided to the joint force in areas like ISR, close air support, air mobility, tactical C2, personnel recovery, and medical evacuation. Much has been accomplished with relatively few assets—and made to look relatively easy in most cases due to a permissive air-threat situation, sufficient basing, and the fairly static nature of associated logistical problems. This operational environment allowed incremental improvements, added by a succession of staffs over time. However, many of the professionals responsible for these improvements have largely moved out of C2 assignments, taking their experience and understanding with them.

The operational C2 environment has been tactically focused on ground operations rather than robust, multidomain campaigns. Although we have trained CHQs with robust scenarios in Blue

Flag and other higher headquarters command post exercieses, funding for those activities has been significantly curtailed or eliminated, with many being cancelled or relegated to "tabletop only" status.[15] We are rapidly approaching a point where some CHQ staff members will never have seen "what right looks like" regarding the full CHQ C2 requirements for high-intensity major combat operations.

We have slowly regressed to simpler processes and products that will not support higher-intensity war fighting, to the detriment of high-level C2 skills. Our total weight of effort in US Central Command's area of responsibility (CENTCOM AOR) has been low enough that we have been able to plan and track the entire ATO using basic Microsoft Office tools. At the same time, our skills with the tools necessary for planning major combat operations via theater battle management core systems applications have atrophied.[16] It has been logical to do so—there is no reason to make a task more difficult during actual combat operations when something less complex works better. However, we need to recognize that the less simplified processes of today may be completely unsuitable to handle more complex issues tomorrow. Now is the appropriate time to challenge ourselves and regain the skills needed for a much higher-demand signal from airpower.

Our ability to conduct C2 has not been significantly contested. Conventional wisdom requires us to consider the likelihood of contested and degraded operations, but we have only recently begun considering their implications for CHQ C2. Currently, we can coordinate the simultaneous actions of military forces around the globe and perform feats of synchronization and precision of which futurists of old could only dream. Allowing ourselves to become more dependent on our tools, we may have lost touch with many of the basic tenets of C2. Articulating the fundamental challenges and trade-offs of C2 across the entire combat air forces (specifically those in operations) will help us take proactive measures to protect our C2 in contested environments. This will also help us avoid the "one size fits all" mentality that never addresses all of the problems involved in a contested and degraded operations scenario.

Threats from Systemic Factors

Because C2 has been "assured" in the conditions described above, an enterprise-level solution has not developed to address some systemic matters that threaten our C2 expertise in terms of managing human capital and resources. We must address eight emerging issues.

C2 demand signals and resource allocations are going in opposite directions. At the very time that more institutional C2 knowledge and experience are needed to deal with near-peer challenges as called for in the Joint Operational Access Concept and supporting concepts like the Air Sea Battle Concept, our C2 resources either remain static or decrease.[17]

C2 experience in the staffs is decreasing because of personnel policies, including the present system of career incentives. A career field for air battle managers in the AWACS and CRC exists, but there is no similar career field at the CHQ C2 level in the Air Force that helps the Air Force Personnel Center match people with the organizational experiences discussed previously with CHQ C2 assignments. Because of the lack of a career field for CHQ C2 operational-level planners—and very few opportunities for squadron command outside a small number of AOC training and testing squadrons—our brightest future leaders (who usually understand the tactical tilt of the Air Force system very well) enjoy few career incentives to seek CHQ C2 assignments actively. Ironically, these AOC and AFFOR assignments would prepare someone for operational and strategic command later as an AFFOR and AOC division director, AOC commander, and JFACC. Instead, these assignments tend to hurt rather than help chances for promotion to senior rank.[18] As a result, those who do attain senior rank usually do so through a succession of mostly tactical assignments or staff assignments other than those in CHQ C2. Often, these officers end up making major decisions that affect the future of the AOC and AFFOR albeit without the full understanding of what CHQs do and what sustaining and modernizing them requires. Talent and intelligence can make up for many deficiencies; the leaders we get through the mandatory path of tactical assignments at the squadron, group, and wing levels usually have those qualities in abundance. However, the development of expertise in a complex enterprise carries fundamental demands for focused engagement with the conceptual elements over time to cultivate intuition, expertise, and mastery. Sometimes there is simply no substitute for time and experience under actual conditions to become truly proficient.[19] When it comes to the complexities of CHQ C2, no crash course can teach personnel all they need to know, no matter how talented the students may be.

C2 is not in our cultural DNA, as are tactical weapons systems. Despite its foundational importance, joint and combined organizational-level C2 is difficult to visualize and even more difficult to fit into service narratives that we use to describe our organizational essence. Good Air Force commanders have traditionally recognized the importance of organizational-level operational C2—hence, the AOC and AFFOR construct. However, few senior leaders have an emotional attachment to C2 in the same way they do airframes, leading to a subtle bias towards the tip-of-the-iceberg systems that most individuals have more familiarity with from their tactical backgrounds. The Air Force's service culture reinforces this propensity to value tactical operations and advanced technologies over operational-level competency.[20] When C2 initiatives have to compete for precious attention and resources, commanders may tend to fall back on the heuristics emphasized by their personal experience in tactical assignments and deemphasize less familiar CHQ programs, even if they are critical to future success from a larger, much more systemic perspective.[21]

Some legacy CHQ C2 training has already fallen victim to budget pressures. AOC initial qualification training has been normalized in the program objective memorandum (POM), but both in-residence advanced AOC training (the Command and Control Warrior Advanced

Course or C2WAC) and initial AFFOR training have been curtailed in recent years because of a lack of funding rather than a lack of demand in the field. Blue Flag, the operational AOC training specifically designed to train AOC, joint air component coordination element (JACCE), and AFFOR personnel in the full range of air tasking cycle processes, has already been cut in fiscal years 2014 and 2015 due to budget pressures, increasing the risk that personnel assigned to the AOC and AFFOR will not experience realistic CHQ C2 battle-rhythm processes until an actual contingency occurs. Emphasis on operational planning has improved in Air Force professional military education (PME) for officers (specifically, Air Command and Staff College), but many officers assigned to AOC and AFFOR staffs do not attend those courses before receiving their AOC, JACCE, and AFFOR assignments. Budget pressures have eliminated CHQ C2 training previously offered by the 505th Command and Control Wing at Hurlburt Field, Florida, to students of the School of Advanced Air and Space Studies despite the high probability that many of its graduates will be assigned to high-impact CHQ C2 jobs after graduation.[22] The service has never offered a formal course to train members of the JACCE, regardless of the critical role they play in connecting higher headquarters and functional component planning with centralized air planning in the JAOC.[23]

Cessation of in-residence AFFOR and advanced training creates systemic effects in the C2 force. When the people selected for these CHQ assignments do not have formal training in the basics, they do the best they can when they get there. They take the initiative and develop procedures on their own that address the exigencies of the particular moment. Nevertheless, these local solutions usually are neither scalable to different levels of intensity nor translatable to other headquarters. Over time, this situation creates a pernicious effect on the aggregate levels of C2 experience and understanding across the force, making adaptation to different situations or combining personnel from various CHQs in an emergency situation a much more intractable problem. The result, validated by our own historical experience before establishment of the CHQ C2 processes, is extended C2 "pickup games" and process disconnects during critical moments of escalation and conflict.

The lack of proper understanding of CHQ C2 and of sufficient doctrinal terminology to distinguish "tip" from "rest" functions creates the illusion that we are adequately addressing C2 from an institutional perspective. Because we don't make a clear doctrinal distinction between the mostly tactical C2 processes in the tip and the mostly bureaucratic C2 processes involved in CHQ C2 in the rest of the iceberg, we tend to talk past each other when we mention C2 generically among different C2-related activities. Sometimes the false impression that "C2 is covered" encourages us to neglect some critical aspects entirely (e.g., CHQ advanced training and career management) in our steady-state budgeting and programming and personnel system. Air battle managers are considered a distinct C2 career field, and many of them later become excellent leaders in CHQ C2 organizations, but their normal duties in the JSTARS, AWACS, and CRC do not specifically prepare them for CHQ assignments or make them CHQ C2 process experts upon initial arrival. POM normalization for AOC initial qualification training has been very beneficial and stabilizing for initial training, but failure to fund the AOC simulation capabilities and their upgrades threatens our ability to provide mission-qualification training once the students leave the schoolhouse.

CHQ C2 systems illiteracy leads directly to strategic illiteracy and service irrelevance. As a distinguished Air Force strategist once remarked, "You're not a strategist unless you're a strategist of bureaucracy."[24] The best strategy is useless unless one understands and knows how to maneuver through the social systems in which strategy is informed, formed into a plan, and transformed into taskings. Further, as the venerable physicist Stephen Hawking once said, "The greatest enemy of knowledge is not ignorance; it is the illusion of knowledge."[25] If leaders rise to rank primarily through demonstrating tactical excellence without the requisite CHQ experience and awareness to understand the relevant issues, they probably will not make the right decisions, no matter how well intentioned, intelligent, or talented they are.

Systemic deficiencies have been concealed by abundant resourcing so far, but that is about to end. In an era of funding for overseas contingency operations, we have often been able to address systemic inattention to CHQ C2 via rapid-acquisition programs and fallout funds. In times of budget austerity, this is less likely to happen. Our ability to create local "bailing wire and paper clip" solutions for C2 technical issues is not going to keep pace with the rate of change as some parts of the C2 system are upgraded through normalized POM inputs while others are neglected.[26]

Faulty C2 Assumptions Caused by Systems Illiteracy

As we explore alternative options to the current AOC and AFFOR constructs in the future, we must be cautious not to oversimplify the problem with proposed solutions that do not acknowledge the full depth of our current C2 processes. Each process has evolved out of necessity to add depth and rigor to the air tasking process, and significant risks may arise if its contributions—and the reasons they were introduced in the first place—are not fully understood. Unless one is truly "systems literate" and considers the whole of the C2 issue before offering simplifying prescriptions, proposals to modify our C2 will probably solve only part of the problem and may make its other parts worse. Knowledge of foundational C2 theory validated by a thorough understanding of history suggests that the following general assumptions about C2 are fundamentally flawed unless they are carefully qualified.

We can automate situational awareness and eliminate the fog of war through technology.[27] Airpower is not just about collecting data, looking for patterns, and selecting the right preprogrammed decision algorithm to activate or deactivate strike packages. It is much more complex, involving an understanding of the entire environment and choosing multiple responses to shape outcomes favorably across the physical, cognitive, and moral domains.[28] In war the desired ends are political effects, which are social constructs by definition. Humans in the loop—more specifically, groups of them working in concert—are still the only parallel processors capable of deducing social context from the results of potential or actual tactical actions.[29] Even the best algorithms behind automated "big data" analysis depend on assumptions built into their search algorithms, ones developed ahead of actual events that may not yield appropriate insights when social contexts change faster than the algorithm can be reprogrammed. Any proposed operational concept that treats air warfare as reducible to a targeting exercise against certain types of targets—and nothing more—is fundamentally flawed from inception.[30]

We can automate the planning process and gain efficiencies in personnel. Blanket information technology solutions, even when well funded, can seldom adapt to very different requirements driven by complex joint and coalition operations. If an automated data-collection process is not configured to "ask" the right questions or the means of displaying information does not match the way that rotating commanders visualize and absorb information, then the tool will actually hinder effective C2. This is a general truth of any complex situation— as the system becomes more complex, "blanket solution" attempts to control them tend to generate more unintended consequences.

We can centralize all of the global requirements for "function X" in one place to gain efficiencies in personnel. Because the social interface prevents full automation of C2 decision making, any C2 system has fundamental human-cognitive load limits. One has only limited time to build the situational awareness and context needed to correctly interpret the information received by humans in the loop. Although it may be possible to centralize some very discrete functions that do not require screening for social context (e.g., weaponeering analysis on discrete target sets or imagery analysis), the artificial intelligence required to do so with the entire C2 enterprise does not yet exist and never will as long as social effects matter. Detailed contextual knowledge is needed to estimate the social effect that airpower actions will have in specific areas and contexts; thus, generalists with wide-area or global responsibilities are less likely to draw correct conclusions looking at the same data as a specialist intimately familiar with local contexts. Air strategy is not simply a matter of hitting targets in a mechanistic fashion—it's about knowing which targets matter in a social sense and why. Consequently, one needs specific area expertise and concentration in areas like geography, economics, local culture, threats, doctrine, and so forth.

We can conduct all of our planning via distributed means. The Air Force learned the importance of "actual presence" the hard way during development of the JACCE, whereby possessing a "seat at the table" became a requirement to have a voice in the plan.[31] This comes down to basic human psychology. We communicate and form trust primarily through receiving nonverbal cues of intent, embodied in what are often unconscious cues passed through gesture and tone of voice, and physical cues that affect our perceptions of trustworthiness in others.[32] Without these, we become suspicious of each other and fill in the missing data with stereotypes that often erode trust and communication. The effect of being on different sleep cycles further reinforces the misperception that distributed planning efforts are not supporting and often run counter to the requirements of war fighters closer to the fight. As anyone who has served in the CENTCOM AOR can attest, it is usually impossible to get anything done with a higher headquarters back home until afternoon, CENTCOM time, and the questions from that headquarters usually arrive at the same time deployed planners are ready to turn in for the night.

We also need to acknowledge that not all critical C2 processes happen during scheduled battle-rhythm events and that having forward planning presence and personal relationships with the key planners is critical to joint planning and execution. Without liaisons and regular battlefield circulation, the air component has less influence in shaping the initial presentation of joint courses of action, which tend to dominate the discussion over subsequent suggestions, even the sounder ones—another documented cognitive bias that is largely subconscious. A final opportunity lost by not having a forward geographic presence is the prospect of chance meetings with planners of the other services. These often lead to better solutions and detection of previously unknown problems that may never surface during preplanned battle-rhythm distributed meetings in which the social pressures of rank and precedence may restrict free discussion or sidebars that often generate the most creative solutions.

Most C2 functions can be distributed to subordinate units and entities. The C2 system necessary to carry out the mission is completely dependent on what the mission is—there is no universal solution for C2. As long as the system can perform the basic strategy-to-task-to-assessment processes described at the beginning of this article and personnel can accomplish their mission in the conditions they encounter, the C2 system is adequate, even without all of the processes in the iceberg. But oftentimes the AOC and AFFOR processes developed the way they did for good reasons. Before options for distribution or consolidation of functions are considered, commanders must understand the impact on their ability to control forces effectively and efficiently when assumptions prove incorrect—when friction and chance enter the equation. Commanders must realize that when they delegate control, they also delegate risk acceptance. If the distributed node does not have the expertise, situational awareness, or span of control necessary to make good command and risk decisions, then delegation of C2 may prove worse than taking an operational pause while the CHQ C2 elements reconstitute their critical processes. This is especially true when joint schemes of maneuver are highly interdependent and when the distributed node is already under stress to perform its primary mission.[33]

"What works in Red Flag and weapons school for C2 training will work for CHQ C2." As we have seen above, the rest of the iceberg gets good training when large organizations have to work with other large organizations and merge their bureaucratic processes in common directions. The tip-of-the-iceberg forces get good training when they have to adapt to changes to a plan that had already been provided in order to fulfill previously defined missions. Thus, with the exception of the combat operations floor, exercise events that usually offer good training for the AOC (conducting parallel planning, racking and stacking priorities, and resolving resource shortfall dilemmas) leave the tactical units spinning uselessly, losing valuable training time while waiting for guidance. It is much better to have a controlled, constructive model for CHQ training in which a simulated air entity can hold endlessly while the staff works through its training objectives and perhaps learns more from a mistake than making the right call in the first place.

Similarly, trying to conduct AOC process training during a tactical exercise with defined takeoff times, airspace, targets, and mandatory lists of players makes it impossible for AOC planners to exercise operational art in a real sense. In real life, the AOC's job is to ask what problems should be solved and design feasible, creative solutions for operational and tactical problems, which may or may not involve all of their assets. Thus, AOC play in a live or virtual event in which players, roles, timing, and locations are defined is analogous to having to define and solve a word problem or receiving an already-solved algebra problem and being told to concoct a story about the variables so that the predetermined flying or simulator schedule solution makes sense. It is good exercise support for the tactical units, but it is not effective CHQ C2 training. If inexperienced AOC personnel serving as AOC response cells (i.e., people who create simulated outputs from processes that aren't really happening to create a realistic training environment for others) don't know "what right looks like," then participation in Red Flag can actually constitute negative training. CHQ training has to do with processes, and CHQ processes do not happen when other headquarters elements are neither participating nor being simulated by someone else.

Having so many outstanding tactical C2 "hammers" in the tip and only a small cadre of identified CHQ C2 experts to consult on new proposals makes it really easy to imagine that all CHQ problems are "nails." Recent proposals for the Advanced Integrated Warfighting Weapons Instructor Course, designed by tactical C2 integration experts to address issues in operational warfare, are going in exactly the *wrong* direction for CHQ C2. Instead of doubling down on tactical experience by requiring participants to spend more time in their specialized family-of-origin major weapons system as tactical integrators, we need to pull tacticians *out* of those systems *sooner* and teach them to be generalist, multidisciplinary CHQ planners and organizational-process experts as senior captains and junior majors.[34] Doing so will give them more time to season in an actual CHQ rather than learn all of their CHQ C2 skills in classrooms and labs. It will allow them to bring real-world CHQ C2 experience into intermediate developmental education and improve their capability to serve later as AOC and AFFOR division chiefs and directors, who need more organizational than tactical skills to perform their CHQ C2 missions.

Six Ways to Secure Operational-Level C2 Excellence

Given the requirements of operational C2 discussed previously and the need for holistic systems literacy to be effective across the entirety of the C2 enterprise, we can make a few general recommendations regarding requirements for maintaining current C2 capabilities in the face of increasing external and internal challenges.

Recognize That CHQ C2 Is Very Challenging and That How Well It Is Done Has a Significant Effect on Strategic Outcomes, with Far-Reaching Consequences for National Security and Prestige

CHQ C2 is not rocket science—it is much more difficult than that. When the hand moves the handle slightly at a component headquarters, the end of the tactical whip can quickly go supersonic. In other high-impact professions that require multidisciplinary knowledge to perform competently, such as medicine or law, we demand extensive screening and professional preparation—including thorough testing and board screening processes—before selecting someone for the task. CHQ C2 should be no different. Assignments there should not be seen as the "alpha tours" of old, a manning bill to be paid and escaped from as soon as possible to maintain career viability in a system biased more towards tactical achievement.

Acknowledge That the Heart of Operational C2 Is a Human Problem, Not a Technical One, Which Requires Specialized Organizational Skills and Practical Experience Earned over Time to Build and Maintain C2 Excellence

The skills necessary at this level are not identical to those required at the tactical level. We must actively encourage and develop dedicated, organizational-level C2 experts with the same rigor as we do at the tactical, identify and track them in the personnel system, and ensure that CHQ C2 experts have career opportunities commensurate with those available to tacticians and strategists. Organizational-level C2 expertise must be multidisciplinary by nature, and those who practice it must have a solid grounding in many different fields of theory and knowledge, as well as the organizational techniques to bring people and insights from various fields into the same planning effort.[35] The background that one needs to perform in the rest of the iceberg includes, but is not limited to, history, geography, decision theory, social and organizational theory, internal and external cultural awareness, awareness of the negative effects of cognitive bias, and familiarity with a number of analytical tools and group-planning techniques that support good decision making.[36] Many of these skills take years of concentrated study before their practitioners become proficient—skills not required or learned in the tactical assignments in which most members begin their career.

We also need to be more proactive in identifying individuals with the aptitude and desire to assume the complex challenges of organizational-level operational C2 and in consciously steering them into viable career paths and command opportunities so they can build the experience they need to lead the C2 enterprise later. This also includes creating squadron-command-equivalent billets within CHQ C2 assignments so that C2 leaders can compete for senior leadership positions later, along with the tactical specialists. It makes no sense to train people specifically for multidisciplinary CHQ C2 positions but then insist that they spend the next four to six years commanding tactically focused units before they can use those skills again, thus allowing their CHQ C2 skills to stagnate in the meantime. It leaves little time for the deliberate engagement and reflection that our future CHQ C2 leaders need to propose innovative CHQ C2 solutions—the current CHQ C2 system is *not* the final answer to our future rest-of-the-iceberg questions.

CHQ C2 assignments should be career enhancements, not speed bumps to avoid. Because these jobs are inherently joint, steering our sharpest young minds towards them will increase our competence— hence, influence—in joint settings as well. The same young officers and noncommissioned officers who rub shoulders with their sister-service equivalents in CHQ C2 assignments will surely see them again someday in a joint headquarters, the Pentagon, and possibly even in the "Tank"—and those personal relationships will pay dividends.[37] If the Air Force wants more say in joint planning and processes, it needs to send Air Force people who can already speak in terms of joint planning processes—not those who are just learning it on the fly after a lifetime as inwardly focused Air Force tactical specialists.

Recognize That Tactical Proficiency in a Specific Mission Design Series and the Ability to "Speak Air Force" Are the Cost of Entry but Are Not Sufficient in Themselves to Succeed at CHQ C2

Simply to survive in joint- and coalition-planning environments, organizational-level operational C2 practitioners must not only be familiar with joint, allied, and sister-service doctrinal concepts and language but also be conversant in several operational-planning methodologies. They must be able to serve as translators between different service languages and cultures, but first they must have proficiency of their own in terms of Air Force doctrine and C2 terminology. They should begin their work in C2 with expertise in at least one or more tactical areas, but they should not stay with one mission design series too long before receiving an operational C2 assignment. This ensures that they have time to develop the organizational skills needed to carry the air tasking cycle all the way from strategy to task. Incentives should be offered to those who pursue sister-service PME after they complete Air Force PME. Allowing people to self-identify themselves for CHQ C2 assignments in such a way is a good indicator of individuals who have the perspicacity and drive to make the dramatic shift from tactics, to operations, and eventually strategy.

Invest in In-Residence Initial and Advanced Training for Organizational-Level Operational C2 Assignments, and Spread Specialized Education across a Career in the Same Way We Do with Our PME

Online AFFOR education is better than nothing, but it robs students of the opportunity to gather valuable insights gleaned from face-to-face interaction with experienced teachers who can tailor their instruction to specific requirements of the students and their assignments. Additionally, spreading out initial and advanced operational-level C2 training—as was the practice between AOC initial qualification training and the Command and Control Warrior Advanced Course—allows students to see a CHQ in action before reengaging in the theory. Doing so leads to a richer educational experience when they return to the classroom and even greater dividends when they become advanced-training graduates. Requiring some experience between initial C2 training and advanced training will better prepare students to engage with the advanced material, and they will even bring back new insights and lessons learned that will strengthen the entire community. CHQ skills require a lifelong-learning mind-set, and our preparations for these positions should mirror this fact. It is good that some of our formal PME courses have already incorporated CHQ C2 education and training into their syllabi, but it is also true that many of the people assigned to CHQ C2 assignments have not yet attended these courses.

Continue to Invest in Organizational CHQ Operational C2 Exercises and Encourage COCOM-Level Exercises to Include Training Objectives That Involve CHQ Processes

Except for people who monitor and direct tactical execution (found mostly in the COD), AOC and AFFOR players get useful mission training when they actually interact with the staffs and entities they would have to talk to in real life to conduct joint and coalition parallel planning, including active participation in joint battle-rhythm processes. Such training can occur in the context of major COCOM exercises like Terminal Fury, Austere Challenge, and Emerald Warrior, as well as Blue Flag, in which those processes can be simulated with enough fidelity to offer AOC personnel accurate inputs and useful critiques of their processes and products to facilitate learning. This does require commitment on the part of the primary training audience—usually the COCOM staff—to create scenarios and master-scenario event lists that address AOC and AFFOR needs since these may be the only opportunities that these entities have to fully exercise their C2 functions in the joint boards, bureaus, centers, and cells that drive a joint battle rhythm.

Explore New Three-Dimensional Operational Graphics, Animations, and Computer Simulations to Raise General Awareness of "Rest of the Iceberg" Issues and to Improve the Systems Literacy of Those Who Are Not C2 Experts but Will Find Themselves Making Decisions about the C2 Enterprise

It is almost impossible to engage either creatively or critically with something without a basic mental model. Rich visualizations and animation have an amazing power to access the creative mind and to inform our intuitions about systemic complexity. Even prespeech infants who do not understand anything about the inner workings of computers can easily manipulate computer interfaces of today to access and play their favorite video games on touch-screen devices using the visual metaphors of Windows-based user interfaces.[38] We have an unprecedented ability to use data to create empirically accurate simulations of operational scenarios. We can and should visually depict our schemes of maneuver, using both rich, multidimensional graphics and simulations to help C2 practitioners better visualize the operational constraints and linkages that make the rest-of-the-iceberg activities especially daunting. This is not to say that we should allow ourselves to be dependent on such tools—the ultimate goal is still to build systemic intuition that can be applied with a grease board as easily as a projector. Currently, however, the products we use are usually too simple for either educating C2 or practicing high-level operational C2. We still employ two-dimensional Microsoft Word and PowerPoint products to frame and war-game complex, multidisciplinary operational problems in the planning process, and we too often present gross oversimplifications of complex planning efforts to decision makers in three-to-four-slide quad-chart decision briefings.

Animated operational graphics that utilize standard symbology—used from initial education through actual mission rehearsals and debriefings—will help us better illustrate joint interdependencies in ways that static, two-dimensional products never can. Using them, we can develop the same kind of intuitive feel for operational warfare that we experience every time we use colored and animated weather maps to evaluate complex weather systems: within just a few seconds of observation, we can usually tell whether or not we need an umbrella. If we had similar visual tools for operational-art concepts, it would be much more difficult to take for granted rest-of-the-iceberg operational considerations like resource allocation and mutual interdependence if the simulation stops when it encounters a constraint. Airpower advocate Alexander de Seversky understood this concept well when he collaborated with Walt Disney in making the film *Victory through Air Power* in 1943. De Seversky used simple, hand-animated operational graphics to illustrate complex concepts of operational art to the general public. Even if his message was at times overly simplistic, the explanatory power of the animations is undeniable and, in many ways, superior to the way we teach the same operational concepts today.[39]

In an ideal situation, we could replace de Seversky's cartoons with accurate, simulator-generated depictions of our operational schemes of maneuver and threats. We could play out an entire joint scheme of maneuver in a simulated battlespace, checking for seams in the plan and limiting operational constraints before presenting joint courses of action to commanders. For example, if a joint plan called for more air-refueling tanker gas than actually available, if the same asset were assigned to multiple locations, or if an asset were planned to penetrate an enemy's integrated air defense system without sufficient mutual support, then the simulation should highlight the discrepancy and point to the limiting factors, in much the same way that commercially available strategy games do with combinations of color and sound alerts. We are already training a generation of gamers to think this way, so why are we not training a generation of planners in a similar fashion?

Are we going to have this kind of modeling and briefing capability soon? No. Would our situational awareness and systemic literacy benefit from the incremental steps it would take to get there, rather than just using the static slides and diagrams we rely on today? Yes. And would it help us to make our planning assumptions explicit and open for debate, even if absolute systemic truth could never be depicted? Absolutely.

Conclusion

Any discussion of icebergs would have to include the tragedy of RMS *Titanic*—the largest, most advanced ship of its time, possessing staggering levels of capacity, technology, prestige, and raw power. Many people, perhaps including some members of its crew, considered it "unsinkable." Of course, they didn't realize the danger presented by icebergs and how little steering command they had with their comparatively small rudder until it was too late.

Photo REmoved Due to Copyright Restrictions

***Titanic* at the docks.** (From Wikimedia Commons, accessed 3 June 2014, http://commons.wikimedia.org/wiki/RMS_Titanic#mediaviewer/File:Titanic.jpg.)

***Titanic*'s stern and rudder.** (From Library of Congress, George Grantham Bain Collection, accessed 3 June 2014, http://www.loc.gov/pictures/item/2001704333/.)

This is not to say that having superior technology and the most impressive gear is undesirable in dangerous environments. Because declining budgets will certainly prompt difficult choices, however, it is crucial to remember that tactical power is useless without sufficient C2 to direct it well. Our service needs a good CHQ C2 rudder and a highly competent crew to direct it in order to avoid leaving Air Force–blue paint marks on an unexpected iceberg someday.[40]

Photo REmoved Due to Copyright Restrictions

Titanic **iceberg**. (From Wikimedia Commons, accessed 3 June 2014, http://commons.wikimedia.org/wiki/File:Theberg.jpg.)

The challenges involved in CHQ C2 and the skill sets needed to execute the plans made there are not the same. The most important way to hedge against future C2 problems is to make sure we maintain—and institutionally value—a deep bench of people who have holistic C2 systems literacy and creatively use the tools available to them to make the needed communication and coordination happen. This means a continued investment in the people, processes, and tools of CHQ C2, lest our tactical excellence be all for naught. ✪

Notes

1. For a detailed description of our current air and space operations center and Air Force forces constructs and planning processes, see Curtis E. LeMay Center for Doctrine Development and Education, "Annex 3-30, Command and Control," 1 June 2007, https://doctrine.af.mil/download.jsp?filename = 3-30-Annex-COMMAND-CONTROL.pdf.

2. For detailed information on Red Flag, see "414th Combat Training Squadron 'Red Flag,'" Nellis Air Force Base, 6 July 2012, http://www.nellis.af.mil/library/factsheets/factsheet .asp?id = 19160.

3. Martin van Creveld, "Command in War: A Historical Overview," in *Advanced Technology Concepts for Command and Control*, ed. Alexander Kott (Philadelphia: Xlibris Corporation, 2004), 27.

4. Joint Publication (JP) 1-02, *Department of Defense Dictionary of Military and Associated Terms*, 8 November 2010 (as amended through 15 March 2014), 45, http://www.dtic.mil /doctrine/new_pubs/jp1_02.pdf.

5. Ibid.

6. Carl H. Builder, Steven C. Bankes, and Richard Nordin, *Command Concepts: A Theory Derived from the Practice of Command and Control* (Santa Monica, CA: RAND, 1998), xiii–xiv, http://www.rand.org/pubs/monograph_reports/MR775.html.

7. The Joint Air Operations Command and Control system and its subordinate systems are described in JP 3-30, *Command and Control for Joint Air Operations*, 10 February 2014, II-7–II-13, http://www.dtic.mil/doctrine/new_pubs/jp3_30.pdf.

8. For a plethora of guides and descriptions on the subject of operational art, see "Air War College Gateway to the Internet," Air University, accessed 3 June 2014, http://www.au.af .mil/au/awc/awcgate/awc-forc.htm#opart.

9. Air Force organizational descriptions can be found in Air Force Instruction 38-101, *Air Force Organization*, 16 March 2011, http://static.e-publishing.af.mil/production/1/af_a1 /publication/afi38-101/afi38-101.pdf. Component major commands are described in par. 2.2.2.2. Component numbered air forces are described in par. 2.2.5.1.

10. Although difficult to find, the most concise description of the AOC is "The CAOC Primer" by Col Dale Shoupe, USAF, retired, a 2008 lesson reading from Air War College. For the official US Air Force description of AOC and AFFOR functions, see Curtis E. LeMay Center for Doctrine Development and Education, *Volume 4, Operations*, 5 June 2013, "Appendix: The Air Operations Center," https://doctrine.af.mil/download.jsp?filename = V4-D31 -Appendix-AOC.pdf.

11. See Curtis E. LeMay Center for Doctrine Development and Education, *Volume 1, Basic Doctrine*, 14 October 2011, "Air Force Component Presentation Considerations," https:// doctrine.af.mil/download.jsp?filename = V1-D45-AF-Presentation-Consider.pdf. See also Curtis E. LeMay Center for Doctrine Development and Education, *Volume 4, Operations*, "Command and Control Mechanisms," https://doctrine.af.mil/download.jsp?filename = V4-D11-C2-mechanisms.pdf.

12. For an excellent discussion of both tip and rest-of-the-iceberg C2 activities and where they fit within the joint concept of "mission command," see Col Dale S. Shoupe, USAF, Retired, "An Airman's Perspective on Mission Command," *Air and Space Power Journal* 26, no. 5 (September–October 2012): 95–108, http://www.airpower.maxwell.af.mil/digital/pdf /articles/2012-Sep-Oct/V-Shoupe.pdf.

13. For a description of the joint operation planning process for air, see JP 3-30, *Command and Control for Joint Air Operations*, III-1–III-15. For information on the joint operations planning process, see JP 5-0, *Joint Operation Planning*, 11 August 2011, chap. 4, http:// www.dtic.mil/doctrine/new_pubs/jp5_0.pdf.

14. These plans include the joint air operations plan (JAOP), air operations directives (AOD), air tasking orders (ATO), AFFOR operation orders (OPORD), and various other subordinate plans, branch plans, and sequel plans.

15. For a description of this exercise, see "Blue Flag," 505th Command and Control Wing, 10 April 2013, http://www.505ccw.acc.af.mil/library/factsheets/factsheet.asp?id=15317.

16. George l. Seffers, "U.S. Air Force Races to Modernize Critical Battle Control System," *Signal Online*, 1 August 2013, http://www.afcea.org/content/?q=node/11453.

17. The Joint Operational Access Concept and its subordinate concepts—the Navy / Air Force–authored Air Sea Battle Concept and the Army / Marine Corps–authored Gaining and Maintaining Access—all call for increased integration among the services, all of which are fundamentally problems that must initially be solved at the JTF and CHQ C2–equivalent level before they are implemented by subordinate C2 nodes in tactical execution. See Department of Defense, *Joint Operational Access Concept (JOAC)*, version 1.0 (Washington, DC: Department of Defense, 17 January 2012), http://www.defense.gov/pubs/pdfs/joac_jan%20 2012_signed.pdf; Air-Sea Battle Office, *Air-Sea Battle: Service Collaboration to Address Anti-Access and Area Denial Challenges* (Washington, DC: Air-Sea Battle Office, May 2013), http:// www.defense.gov/pubs/ASB-ConceptImplementation-Summary-May-2013.pdf; and US Army and US Marine Corps, *Gaining and Maintaining Access: An Army–Marine Corps Concept* (Washington, DC: US Army and US Marine Corps, March 2012), http://www.defense innovationmarketplace.mil/resources/Army%20Marine%20Corp%20Gaining%20and%20 Maintaining%20Access.pdf.

18. One must be a squadron, group, and wing commander to become a general officer. Thus, many of the people who have to pass through these wickets and still make the necessary gates and timing can afford to spend only a single-year or two-year tour at the most on the way up the chain. There are no squadron command opportunities in CHQ that I am aware of outside the 505th Command and Control Wing assignments, and personnel are still nominated for command by their old major weapons system porch. Consequently, if individuals go to an AOC or AFFOR as majors, there's a good chance that they are alienating the people who would otherwise have to choose them for that crucial squadron command position at a sufficiently young age to be marked off for possible wing command track.

19. For an excellent summary of some of the latest research on building expertise and mastery, see Dan Goleman, *Focus: The Hidden Driver of Excellence* (New York: Harper, 2013); and Gary Klein, *Streetlights and Shadows: Searching for the Keys to Adaptive Decision Making* (Cambridge, MA: MIT Press, 2009).

20. For the classic analysis of Air Force service culture, as well as an analysis of the institutional ethos of all of the US military services, see Carl Builder, *The Masks of War: American Military Styles in Strategy and Analysis* (Baltimore: John Hopkins University Press, 1989).

21. See Gary Klein, *Sources of Power: How People Make Decisions* (Cambridge, MA: MIT Press, 1998).

22. The mission of the School of Advanced Air and Space Studies is to "Educate strategists for the Air Force and the Nation." See "About SAASS," School of Advanced Air and Space Studies, accessed 3 June 2014, http://usafsaass.blogspot.com/p/about-saass.html. Thus, the decision to curtail C2 training to focus on larger strategy issues in an era of budget austerity is both in line with SAASS's primary emphasis and appropriate. The school's curriculum does include operational-level warfare concepts in its lessons, providing some engagement with CHQ C2 concepts. The primary gap left by the curtailment of 505th Com-

mand and Control Wing training is the chance for SAASS students to engage with highly experienced JFACC senior mentors and the Operational Command Training Program instructors, who collectively have centuries of CHQ C2 experience. They are also current on worldwide CHQ C2 configurations due to their frequent rotations into the field conducting exercise support. The larger issue with C2 education is the systemic one beyond the scope of SAASS. The Air Force does not make expertise in operational C2 a prerequisite—or even preferred—to attend SAASS, despite the fact that many of its graduates will be expected to lead joint and Air Force planning efforts as operational planning team leads in their "payback" assignments. In the latter, they will work side by side with graduates of the School of Advanced Military Studies, School of Advanced Warfighting, Maritime Advanced Warfighting School, and Joint Advanced Warfighting School who have been specifically trained in higher-headquarters-level C2 planning processes. Thus, there is an expectation of CHQ C2 proficiency in SAASS graduates in the field and in the personnel system but no guarantee that they will possess it when they arrive at CHQ C2 assignments as operational planning team leads or division directors.

23. For a brief description of the evolution of the air component coordination element, which will be referred to as the joint air component coordination element in future doctrine documents, see Maj Gen Kenneth S. Wilsbach and Lt Col David J. Lyle, "NATO Air Command–Afghanistan: The Continuing Evolution of Airpower Command and Control," *Air and Space Power Journal* 28, no. 1 (January–February 2014): 11–25, http://www.airpower .maxwell.af.mil/digital/pdf/articles/2014-Jan-Feb/SLP-Wilsbach-Lyle.pdf.

24. Dr. Tom Ehrhard (remarks during the School of Advanced Air and Space Studies "Grad Jam," Maxwell AFB, AL, Spring 2011).

25. Nola Taylor Redd, "Stephen Hawking Biography," Space.com, 30 May 2012, http:// www.space.com/15923-stephen-hawking.html.

26. Not to be taken literally, this is a common expression used by people forced to adapt various program-of-record C2 systems to non-program-of-record systems that are not designed or upgraded together. This usually results in disconnects between the C2 systems used for mission accomplishment and the constructive simulations of real-world inputs, such as radar feeds and message traffic during C2 training. Additionally, cross-domain security-level transfer issues often must be overcome creatively when working with different CHQ C2 entities. Despite the existence of baseline AOC systems, each AOC adapts to fit its particular local situation (including establishing connectivity with host nation and coalition forces), so each training event requires unique information technology solutions to facilitate it. The further that program-of-record systems advance compared to the training and testing systems with which they must connect, the more challenging becomes the prospect of keeping the systems compatible.

27. This is overreach typically ascribed to those advocating approaches based on the philosophy of network-centric warfare, best described in ADM A. K. Cebrowski, *The Implementation of Network Centric Warfare* (Washington, DC: Department of Defense, Office of Force Transformation, 5 January 2005), http://www.carlisle.army.mil/DIME/documents/oft _implementation_ncw%5B1%5D.pdf. See also publications by the Department of Defense's C4ISR Cooperative Research Program, such as David S. Alberts, John J. Garstka, and Frederick P. Stein, *Network Centric Warfare: Developing and Leveraging Information Superiority*, 2nd ed. rev. (Washington, DC: CCRP, 2000), http://www.dodccrp.org/files/Alberts_NCW.pdf; and David S. Alberts and Richard E. Hayes, *Power to the Edge: Command . . . Control . . . in the In-*

formation Age (Washington, DC: CCRP, 2005), http://www.dodccrp.org/files/Alberts _Power.pdf. For the most current CCRP documents, see "The Command and Control Research Program," accessed 3 June 2014, http://www.dodccrp.org/.

28. Using three domains to approximate reality has many historical antecedents, including versions by Plato through J. F. C. Fuller and John Boyd. For the purposes of this article, the domains are defined as follows: physical domain (the physical artifacts of the world, including the earth, ourselves, our tools, and the electromagnetic spectrum); cognitive domain (the means by which we process information from the physical world through a combination of individual neurobiological processes, social interaction, and interaction with the physical domain using various forms of information technologies; this also includes the subconscious processing of information in the human brain); moral domain (the uniquely human domain that defines the personal and collective meanings of the information we process in the cognitive domain; this includes the conscious portion of human thought and memory that interprets the various signals produced in the cognitive domain and gives them meaning in a social sense). For more explanation, see Lt Col David J. Lyle, "Complexity, Neuroscience, Networks, and Violent Extremism: Foundations for an Operational Approach," in *Tools for Operational Considerations: Insights from Neurobiology and Neuropsychology on Influence and Extremism—An Operational Perspective*, ed. Col Marty Reynolds and Lt Col David Lyle (Washington, DC: Joint Chiefs of Staff, April 2013), 64–65, http://nsiteam .com/scientist/wp-content/uploads/2014/02/Influence-and-Extremism-White-Paper -Approved-for-Public-Release-30Apr13v3R.pdf.

29. For a discussion of sociological factors pertaining to operational C2 in CHQ C2 settings, see Dr. Hriar Cabayan et al., eds., *Humans in the Loop: Validation and Validity Concepts in the Social Sciences in the Context of Applied and Operational Settings*, Strategic Multilayer Assessment Occasional White Paper (Washington, DC: Joint Chiefs of Staff, August 2013), http://nsiteam.com/scientist/wp-content/uploads/2014/02/U_Social-Science-II-White -Paper-Approved-for-Public-Release-26Aug13.pdf.

30. For a typical critique of network-centric warfare and concepts deriving from it, see Thomas P. M. Barnett, "The Seven Deadly Sins of Network Centric Warfare," US Naval Institute *Proceedings* 125, no. 1 (January 1999): 36–39, http://www.usni.org/magazines /proceedings/1999-01/seven-deadly-sins-network-centric-warfare. See also Mary Sterpka King, "Preparing the Instantaneous Battlespace: A Cultural Examination of Network-Centric Warfare," *Topia*, nos. 23–24 (2010): 304–29, http://pi.library.yorku.ca/ojs/index.php/topia /article/view/31834. For an excellent critical analysis of the systems thinking behind the concepts of network-centric warfare, see Sean T. Lawson, *Nonlinear Science and Warfare: Chaos, Complexity, and the US Military in the Information Age* (New York: Routledge, 2014).

31. A popular saying among forward planning elements, "virtual presence equals actual absence," reflects a perception problem that CHQ C2 headquarters constantly have unless they also possess effective liaisons placed forward to provide the "actual presence." See Wilsbach and Lyle, "NATO Air Command–Afghanistan," for a brief description of the evolution of the air component coordination element, which will be referred to as the joint air component coordination element in future doctrine documents.

32. The most significant revelations in recent cognitive neuroscience are not that we have unconscious processes that drive conscious thought; rather, they reflect the realization that we have very little conscious access to them in most cases. Several notable, recent works summarize some of these findings at a level accessible to the general reader; the most no-

table is *Thinking Fast and Slow* by Nobel Laureate economist Daniel Kahneman (New York: Farrar, Strauss, and Giroux, 2011). See also David Eagleman, *Incognito: The Secret Lives of the Brain* (New York: Random House, 2011); Duncan J. Watts, *Everything Is Obvious (Once You Know the Answer): How Common Sense Fails Us* (New York: Crown Business, 2011); Shankar Vendantam, *The Hidden Brain: How Our Unconscious Minds Elect Presidents, Control Markets, Wage Wars, and Save Our Lives* (New York: Spiegel and Grau, 2010); and Michael S. Gazzaniga, *Who's in Charge? Free Will and the Science of the Brain* (New York: HarperCollins, 2011).

33. See the discussion of C2 systems "coupling" in Lt Col Michael Kometer, *Command in Air War: Centralized versus Decentralized Control of Combat Airpower* (Maxwell AFB, AL: Air University Press, June 2007), 60–62, http://www.au.af.mil/au/aupress/digital/pdf/book/b_0107_kometer_command_air_war.pdf.

34. The advanced integrated war-fighting concept calls for 10 years in the primary Air Force specialty code and 120 months of operational flying duty accumulation (OFDA) for aircrews before attending the Advanced Integrated Warfighting Weapons Instructor Course, including three years of instructor experience in their family-of-origin tactical weapons system. Instead, personnel showing interest and promise for CHQ C2 should be allowed to leave with 100 months OFDA and serve in AFFOR and AOC positions after seven years of flying. Doing so will allow them to gain between two and four years of CHQ C2 experience and remain competitive for intermediate developmental education attendance, including participation in the Advanced Studies Group programs (School of Advanced Air and Space Studies [SAASS], School of Advanced Military Studies [SAMS], School of Advanced Warfighting [SAW], Marine Advanced Warfighting School [MAWS]) along normal timelines.

35. The benefits of multidisciplinary approaches to problem solving are detailed in Steven Johnson's *Where Good Ideas Come From: The Natural History of Innovation* (New York: Riverhead Books, 2010); and Scott E. Page's *The Difference: How the Power of Diversity Creates Better Groups, Firms, Schools, and Societies* (Princeton, NJ: Princeton University Press, 2007).

36. For an excellent discussion of individual and group biases that influence decision making, see Richards J. Heuer Jr., *Psychology of Intelligence Analysis* (McLean, VA: Center for the Study of Intelligence, Central Intelligence Agency, 1999), https://www.cia.gov/library/center-for-the-study-of-intelligence/csi-publications/books-and-monographs/psychology-of-intelligence-analysis/PsychofIntelNew.pdf; Strategic Multilayer Assessment Editorial Board, *From the Mind to the Feet: Assessing the Perception-to-Intent-to-Action Dynamic* (Maxwell AFB, AL: Air University Press, 2011), http://www.au.af.mil/au/awc/awcgate/afri/from_the_mind_to_the_feet.pdf; and Dylan Evans, *Risk Intelligence: How to Live With Uncertainty* (New York: Free Press, 2012). For a detailed description of multiframe referencing in operational processes, see Dr. Chris Paparone, *The Sociology of Military Science: Prospects for Postinstitutional Military Design* (New York: Bloomsbury, 2013).

37. It is highly likely that the field grade officers who serve as joint planners during the contingencies of today will end up being the O-6s and general/flag officers of tomorrow. Building strong personal relationships over years can only improve trust and honest dealing when institutional preferences clash in the future, ultimately resolved by the most senior officers making decisions in places like the "Tank," where the members of the Joint Chiefs of Staff use their staffs' recommendations to collectively make decisions that affect the entire joint force. Anecdotally, the author challenges the reader to find any senior leader with experience in either situation who will say that personal relationships with members from the other services were not critical to achieving positive outcomes.

38. For an excellent presentation on the power of visualization, see the TED (Technology, Entertainment, and Design) talk by David McCandless, "The Beauty of Data Visualization," video, 17:56, July 2010, http://www.ted.com/talks/david_mccandless_the_beauty_of _data_visualization; and Eric Berlow, "Simplifying Complexity," video, 3:42, TED, July 2010, http://www.ted.com/talks/eric_berlow_how_complexity_leads_to_simplicity. For a study of using visualization for campaign planning, see MAJ Richard D. Paz, "Visualizing War: Visual Technologies and Military Campaign Planning," research paper (Fort Leavenworth, KS: US Army Command and General Staff College, 2003), http://www.au.af.mil/au/awc/awcgate /army/visualizing_war.pdf.

39. Review of *Victory through Air Power* by Alexander de Seversky (Disney Studios), 1943, Youtube video, 1:05:20, accessed 16 May 2014, http://www.youtube.com/watch?v=J7Nj J59bf0M/.

40. Alasdair Wilkins, "What Happened to the Iceberg That Sank the Titanic?," *Wired*, 16 April 2012, http://www.wired.com/2012/04/titanic-iceberg-history//.

Lt Col Dave Lyle, USAF

Lieutenant Colonel Lyle (USAFA; MBA, Louisiana Tech; MMAS, US Army Command and General Staff College; MAAS, School of Advanced Air and Space Studies) has recently been assigned to the Curtis E. LeMay Center for Doctrine Development and Education, Maxwell AFB, Alabama. He has served in various assignments related to command and control in the past 10 years, including air and space operations center (AOC) assignments at the 613 AOC and combined air operations center; Pacific Air Forces Inspector General AOC inspector; director of operations for the 505th Combat Training Squadron; various assignments in joint air component coordination elements, including serving as the A-5 (Strategic Plans) of the 9th Air and Space Expeditionary Task Force– Afghanistan in Kabul; and director of staff for the 505th Command and Control Wing, Hurlburt Field, Florida. He was an AOC initial qualification training honor graduate and Command and Control Warrior Advanced Course graduate, holding US Army qualifications as a joint planner and distinguished master strategist. A master navigator with more than 2,400 flying hours in the B-52H, Lieutenant Colonel Lyle flew 43 combat missions over Kosovo and Afghanistan.